Skylights

William K. Durr
Jean M. LePere
John J. Pikulski

Consultant:
Hugh Schoephoerster

HOUGHTON MIFFLIN COMPANY   **BOSTON**

Atlanta   Dallas   Geneva, Illinois   Hopewell, New Jersey   Palo Alto   Toronto

Acknowledgments

Grateful acknowledgment is given for the contributions of Paul McKee.

For each of the selections listed below, grateful acknowledgment is made for permission to adapt and/or reprint copyrighted material, as follows:

"Amy for Short," adapted from *Amy for Short,* by Laura Joffe Numeroff. Copyright © 1976, Laura Joffe Numeroff. Adapted with permission of Macmillan Publishing Co., Inc.

"As Soon As It's Fall," from *Cricket in a Thicket,* by Aileen Fisher. Copyright © 1963 by Aileen Fisher. Reprinted by permission of Charles Scribner's Sons.

"At Mrs. Appleby's," by Elizabeth Upham McWebb. Reprinted from *Child Life* magazine, copyright © 1945. Reprinted by permission of the author.

"Big Boss," adapted from *Big Boss,* by Anne Rockwell. Copyright © 1975 by Anne Rockwell. Adapted with permission of Macmillan Publishing Co., Inc., and Curtis Brown, Ltd.

"Caterpillars," from *Cricket in a Thicket,* by Aileen Fisher. Copyright © 1963 by Aileen Fisher. Reprinted by permission of Charles Scribner's Sons.

"Choosing," by Eleanor Farjeon. Copyright 1933, © renewed 1961 by Eleanor Farjeon. From *Poems for Children,* by Eleanor Farjeon. Copyright 1951 by Eleanor Farjeon. Reprinted by permission of J.B. Lippincott Company and Harold Ober Associates.

"Clarence and the Burglar," adapted from *Clarence and the Burglar,* by Patricia Lauber. Copyright © 1973 by Patricia Lauber. (Adapted by F.N. Monjo from *Clarence the TV Dog.*) Adaptation by permission of Coward, McCann and Geoghegan, Inc. and John Schaffner, Literary Agent.

"Do You Have the Time, Lydia?" from the book *Do You Have the Time, Lydia?* by Evaline Ness. Copyright © 1971 by Evaline Ness. Reprinted by permission of E. P. Dutton & Co., Inc. and The Bodley Head.

"Escalators," by Candice Taylor, from *Poems and Verses About the City;* Copyright 1968 by Bowmar/Noble Publishers, Inc. Used by permission of Bowmar/Noble Publishers, Inc., Los Angeles, California.

"The Folk Who Live in Backward Town," from *Hello and Good-by,* by Mary Ann Hoberman. Copyright © 1959 by Mary Ann Hoberman. Reprinted by permission of Russell & Volkening, Inc. as agents for the author.

"The Garden," from *Frog and Toad Together,* by Arnold Lobel. Copyright © 1971, 1972 by Arnold Lobel. Reprinted by permission of Harper & Row, Publishers, Inc. British rights granted by World's Work Ltd.

(Acknowledgments and Artist Credits are continued on page 272.)

Contents

Skylights

MAGAZINE ONE

Contents

Big Boss

by ANNE ROCKWELL

A tiger was going through the forest.
He said, "I am a big, hungry tiger. And I want
something to eat!"

But the tiger could not find anything to eat
in the forest.

At last he came to a river. He looked
at himself in the river and smiled.
"What a beautiful tiger I am," he said.
"I am a big, hungry, beautiful tiger.
And I want something good to eat."

Just then the tiger saw a little green frog.

"You look like something good to eat," said the tiger to the frog. "You are very small. But you will do."

"Oh, I would not eat me up if I were you," said the frog. "For I am the Big Boss of this forest." And the frog smiled.

9

"You don't look like a Big Boss
to me," said the tiger. "You look like
a little green frog. I don't believe you."
"Don't believe me, then," said the frog.
"But if you eat me up, you will be in trouble."
"Trouble?" asked the tiger. "What trouble?"
"Big trouble," said the frog. "For I am
the Big Boss of the forest."

The tiger thought for a while. Then he said, "Listen. Show me just one thing you can do better than I can. I know you can't jump as far as I can. You will see."

Then the tiger said, "We will jump over the river and land on the other side. If I jump farther than you, I will eat you up. If you jump farther than I, you can jump away. How is that?"

"All right," said the frog. "But you will see. No one can jump farther than the Big Boss!"

And the two of them got ready to jump.

Just as the tiger jumped, the little frog
jumped onto the tiger's tail. He stayed there
while the tiger jumped over the river.

Just as the tiger got to the other side
of the river, the frog let go. He jumped
over the tiger's head. He landed right
in front of the tiger.

"You see," said the frog, "I told you I would win."

"Yes, you did win," said the tiger. "But I am still hungry. So I will eat you anyway!"

"Oh, no you won't," said the frog. And he jumped under a leaf.

The frog was as green as the leaf. The tiger could not see the frog. But he could hear him laughing as he jumped far, far away.

Animal Coloring

What do you see when you look
at this picture? Do you see rocks?
Take another look. There is a bird
hiding there.

Many animals have coloring that helps
them to hide. This bird's coloring is
very much like the colors of the rocks.
That is why it is hard to see the bird.

These tigers are looking for something
to eat. They are waiting in the field
of grass. A tiger's stripes help it
to hide in the grass.

Spots can make animals hard to find, too.
This little deer is hiding in the leaves.
The deer's brown coloring and
white spots help it
to hide.

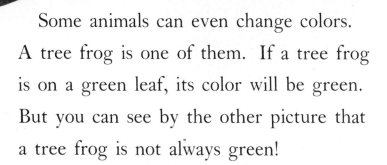

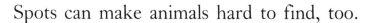

Some animals can even change colors.
A tree frog is one of them. If a tree frog
is on a green leaf, its color will be green.
But you can see by the other picture that
a tree frog is not always green!

Another animal that changes its color is
the snowshoe rabbit. The snowshoe rabbit
is brown in the summer. It is hard to see
the rabbit as it runs over the ground.
In the winter, the snowshoe rabbit's color
changes. It is hard to see a white rabbit
on white snow.

Look at the leaves in this picture.
Are they all leaves, or is something
hiding there?

Did you see just one butterfly?
Look again, very carefully. There are
three butterflies in the picture!

The next time
you see a plant or a leaf,
look very carefully.
You may be seeing
an animal, too.

The Talking Tiger

by ARNOLD SPILKA

If a tiger

Walks beside you

And he whispers:

"Where are you going?"

Do not answer,

Just keep walking

Just keep walking, walking, walking.

And if he continues talking
You keep walking.
Let him talk.
You just walk.
A talking tiger
Never bites,
A walking tiger
Never fights.
But if you find
That he's a bore
Then go right home
And shut the door.

Grownups Are Funny

by LILIAN MOORE

"Grownups are funny," thought Ramon.
"It is so nice here. Why would they want
to move to an apartment house?"

"Do not be sad, Ramon," said his mother.

"But I like it here in Grandfather's house," said Ramon.

"You will like the apartment house, too," said his father.

"Many people live there!" said Aunt Rosa. She looked very happy.

When he said good-by to Grandfather's cat, Ramon wanted to cry.

Ramon gave the cat a big hug and said, "Good-by, Big Pedro."

And Big Pedro said, "Meow!"

The apartment house had many floors
and many children.

Ramon's apartment was 3A.

Jimmy lived on the top floor in Apartment 5B.

Leon lived in Apartment 4C.

Johnny and his sister Lola lived
right next door to Ramon.

And Sara and Sammy lived right under Ramon
in Apartment 2A.

There was always someone to play with.

Mr. Carlos took care of the apartment house.
He lived with a big gray cat called Misty.

When Ramon saw her, he thought of Big Pedro
and gave her a big hug.

Misty said, "Meow."

After that, Ramon and Misty and Mr. Carlos
were friends. Sometimes Mr. Carlos let Ramon
feed Misty.

"I wish you were my cat!" he told her.

One day Ramon's mother took him
to get new sneakers.

As soon as they got home, Ramon ran
to Apartment 5B.

"Hello, Ramon," said Jimmy's mother.
"Jimmy went down to call for Leon."

Ramon ran down to Apartment 4C.

"Hello, Ramon," said Leon's father.
"Leon and Jimmy went to call for Johnny
and Lola."

Johnny and Lola had called for Sammy
and Sara. But no one was there now.

Ramon ran outside. "Where is everybody?"
He had nobody to show his new sneakers to now.

He sat down on the steps and that was where Mr. Carlos found him.

"Hello," said Mr. Carlos. "What are you doing *here,* Ramon?"

"I came to find somebody to play with," said Ramon, "but I can't find *anybody!*"

"They are all looking at something," said Mr. Carlos.

"Looking at what?" asked Ramon.

"Come and see."

Mr. Carlos went into his apartment.
Ramon went with him.

Then Ramon saw his friends. And he saw
what they were looking at.

Misty was in a box and with her were
three little kittens.

"Oh!" cried Ramon. He ran to the box.

"Look at the little white one!" said Jimmy.
"That's the one I like best."

"I like the black one," said Leon.

"And you, Ramon?" asked Mr. Carlos.

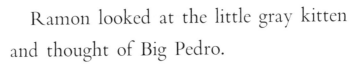

Ramon looked at the little gray kitten
and thought of Big Pedro.

"I like that one," he said.

"How little they are!" said Sara.

"They will soon be big," said Mr. Carlos.
"They will be running into everything.
After that, I have to give them away."

"Give them away!" cried the children.

"I can't keep all these cats,"
said Mr. Carlos. "The black one is
for my friend down the street.
The white one is for my sister."

Ramon looked at the little gray kitten.

"And that one?" he asked.

Mr. Carlos laughed. "Misty says
that kitten is for Ramon."

That night Ramon told his mother and father
and Aunt Rosa all about the kitten.

"I will call him *Little* Pedro," said Ramon.

"I will see *Big* Pedro soon," said Aunt Rosa.
"I am going back to Grandfather's house
to live."

Ramon looked at her in surprise.

"I don't like it here," said Aunt Rosa.
"An apartment house is too big.
Too many people."

Ramon shook his head. "It is so nice here,"
he thought. "And Aunt Rosa is moving away.
Grownups are funny."

What I'd Like

by LEE BLAIR

One or two ponies,
    One or two dogs;
Two or three hamsters,
    Two or three frogs;
Three or four turtles,
    Three or four fish;
Four or five crickets,
        Grasshoppers,
        Tadpoles,
        Butterflies,
        Angleworms,
        Lightning bugs
        Hopping toads —
That is my wish!

Thinking the Right Meaning

Read these two sentences. As you read
each one, decide which picture it goes with.

1. Sue's dog has a brown **spot** on its head.
2. This is a good **spot** to put a doghouse.

The word spot does not have the same
meaning in the two sentences you read.
But you could tell what meaning was right
for each one. The other words in the sentence
helped you.

Below are the same two sentences. You can see that there is a line under some of the words in each sentence. Look carefully at those words. Those are the words that help you think of the right meaning for the word <u>spot</u> in each sentence.

Sue's <u>dog</u> has a <u>brown</u> spot <u>on its head</u>.
This is a <u>good</u> spot <u>to put a doghouse</u>.

Many words have more than one meaning. If you do not think the right meaning, the sentence will not make sense. That's why you have to be sure that you think the right meaning for a word.

The word <u>coat</u> has more than one meaning.
Think about the meaning <u>coat</u> has
in this sentence:

3. Ned put the first **coat** of paint
   on the house.

Now look at the pictures below.
Which picture does the sentence go with?
Which words in the sentence helped you
to know that?

If the first meaning you think of
for a word does not make sense, read
the sentence again. Think of a meaning
that does make sense in the sentence.

In the sentences below, each word in heavy black letters has more than one meaning. Use the other words in the sentence to help you think of the right meaning for each of those words.

4. The boat will **land** near that rock.
5. All the **land** up to that tree is ours.

6. It was **hard** to see through the snow.
7. The ground was **hard** all winter.

8. Ted had some **change** in his pocket.
9. Sara wants to **change** places with me.

10. There was a small **light** on by the door.
11. The animal had **light** and dark stripes.

The Rabbit and the Turnip

translated by RICHARD SADLER

It was a cold winter morning. And there was snow on the ground. Little Rabbit went out to look for food. He found two turnips. He ate up one of them.

Then he said, "It is snowing so hard, and it is so cold. Little Donkey may have nothing to eat. I will take my other turnip to him."

He ran to Little Donkey's house at once. But Little Donkey was out. So Little Rabbit left the turnip at Little Donkey's doorstep. Then he went back home.

Now, Little Donkey had gone out to look
for food. He found a potato. When he
got home and saw the turnip, he was
very surprised. "Who could have put it
there?" he thought.

Then he said to himself, "It is snowing
so hard, and it is so cold. Maybe
Little Sheep has nothing to eat. I will
take it to her."

He took the turnip to Little Sheep's house.
But there was no sign of Little Sheep. So
he left the turnip on Little Sheep's table.
Then he ran back home.

Meanwhile, Little Sheep had been looking
for food. She had found a cabbage
and was running home to eat it.

When she got to her house and found
the turnip, she was surprised. Who could
have put it there? Little Sheep thought she
should give the turnip to Little Deer.
It was snowing so hard, and it was so cold.
She felt sure Little Deer would be hungry.

So Little Sheep took the turnip
to Little Deer's house. But there was
no one at home. So she left the turnip
on Little Deer's chair and went home.

Now, it so happened that Little Deer
was out looking for food. She found
some nice green leaves. She, too, was
very surprised to find the turnip waiting
for her at home.

"I will give this beautiful turnip
to Little Rabbit," she said to herself.
"It is snowing so hard, and it is so cold.
Maybe he has nothing to eat."

Little Deer ran to Little Rabbit's house
at once. And there was Little Rabbit,
fast asleep. Little Deer did not want
to wake him up. So she pushed the turnip
inside the door and went away.

When Little Rabbit got up and found
the turnip, he thought he must be dreaming.
He said to himself, "How nice of someone
to give me this turnip!"

And he ate it all up.

As Soon As It's Fall

by AILEEN FISHER

Rabbits and foxes
as soon as it's fall
get coats that are warm
with no trouble at all,
coats that are furry
and woolly and new,
heavy and thick
so the cold can't get through.

They don't have to buy them
or dye them or try them,
they don't have to knit them
or weave them or fit them,
they don't have to sew them
or stitch them all through,

They just have to *grow* them,
and that's what they do.

Do You Have the Time, Lydia?

by EVALINE NESS

Once there was a little girl named Lydia.
She lived with her father, who grew flowers,
and Andy, who was her brother.

Every day Lydia's father was busy
in his greenhouse, where the plants got
so big they needed holes in the roof.

Every day Lydia was busy painting pictures,
reading books, and making things. Lydia was
so busy doing so many things she never
finished anything.

Andy could do some things, but some things
he didn't know how to do. If he asked Lydia
to help him do something, she always said,
"No-no-no-no! I haven't got time!"

Whenever her father heard Lydia say that,
he always said, "Oh no? Oh ho! If you
take time, you can have time."

But Lydia was too busy to listen.

Andy liked to play on the beach.
One morning on the beach he found an old
lobster trap. He brought it home and
into Lydia's room. She sat making something
for the cat.

"Look!" he shouted. "A racing car! Will you
fix it for me, Lydia? Then I can be
in Dr. Arnold's race. I can win a dog!"

Without looking up, Lydia said, "No-no-no-no!
I haven't got time!"

"The race is today!" cried Andy.

Lydia stopped working long enough to look at the trap. "Well, all right. I'll fix it," she said. "But not now."

"You don't care!" cried Andy.

"I said I'd fix it, didn't I?" said Lydia.

Andy looked at Lydia for a long time. Then he backed out of the room.

Lydia stopped what she was doing and found her skates. She put the wheels from her skates on the trap. Then she cut two big headlights out of paper and put them on the front of the trap. She used a box to make a seat.

"Good!" said Lydia. "All it needs now is a steering wheel. And I know just where to find one!"

Lydia ran to the garage. On a table
in the garage was an old wheel. As Lydia went
to get it, she saw a big bowl on the floor.

"All that needs," said Lydia,
"is a little water and some fish.
And I know just where to find them!"

Away Lydia raced — down to the boathouse
to get her fishing net.

The first thing she saw there was
her father's boat full of water. Lydia found
a can in the boathouse and began to take
out the water. But the more she took out,
the more water came in. Lydia ran up the beach
to the greenhouse to tell her father.

Take Time, Have Time

Before Lydia got to the greenhouse, she stopped. Near the water was a sea gull. Its eyes were shut. One of its wings was hurt.

"You need help!" shouted Lydia. "And I know just where to find it!"

She began to run. She ran all the way to Dr. Arnold's house. But Dr. Arnold wasn't home. On the door was a note: BACK SOON. AT THE RACE.

The race!

Up the street ran Lydia. At the top of the hill she came to a stop. There was Andy. The race was over. All the cars were at the bottom of the hill. Dr. Arnold was just giving a spotted dog to the winner.

Andy looked at Lydia. Then he turned
and ran.

"Andy!" cried Lydia. "I was fixing it.
But I didn't have enough time!"

Andy ran on. He didn't look back.

Lydia walked back to Dr. Arnold's house.
She sat down on the doorstep and cried
and cried. Then she stopped, because she
couldn't cry anymore.

Someone said, "Well! Have you finished
your crying?"

Lydia looked up and saw Dr. Arnold.
"Yes," said Lydia, "I did take time
to finish *something*."

"Now what?" asked Dr. Arnold.

Then Lydia thought of the sea gull.

"The sea gull!" she shouted. "Dr. Arnold! It's hurt. It's on the beach. It can't fly!

"Come on!" she called as she ran to the beach.

At last they were there, and there was the sea gull.

Dr. Arnold gave the gull something to make it sleep. Then he fixed its wing.

"This bird is going to be all right," said Dr. Arnold. "But it can't fly for a while. Why don't you take the gull home, Lydia, and feed it a nice big fish? That is, if you have enough time."

Lydia looked down at the sleeping sea gull.

"Oh ho! I'll take time!" said Lydia.

After Dr. Arnold left, Lydia took
the gull home.

She made a bed for it in the bottom
of a basket. Then she carefully placed
the gull on its bed.

Lydia took the sea gull in its basket
and placed it in front of Andy.

"Andy," said Lydia. "Look what I found
for you."

Andy looked at the gull. He said nothing.

"Did you know that dogs can't fly?"
asked Lydia.

Andy said, "I don't want your old bird."

Lydia left the sea gull with Andy.
Then she went back to the garage. She got
the old wheel from the table.

As she was leaving the garage, Lydia spotted
a birdhouse. It was one she had started
to make a long time ago. All it needed
was a roof.

"What that birdhouse needs —" began Lydia.
She stopped. She looked at the wheel
in her hand. "What that birdhouse needs
is nothing!"

Lydia raced out of the garage and
into the house to her room.

She had just finished fixing the steering wheel
in place when someone said, "I don't want
your old trap."

"Oh, Andy!" cried Lydia. "Yes, you do, too!
I'll paint it red and put a bell on it!"

Andy thought about it.

"Will it have a ladder?" he asked.

"A ladder, too!" cried Lydia.

"But you don't have enough time," said Andy.

"Oh no? Oh ho! If I take time, I can
have time!" said Lydia.

Did You Know?

There is an animal called the flying squirrel. But it cannot really fly. It got that name because it looks as if it is flying as it goes from tree to tree.

This bird cannot fly. But it can get around in another way.

Some flowers can be very big. You can tell
how big this flower is by seeing it next to
two flowers you know.

Point of View

by DAVID McCORD

The little bat hangs upside down,
And downside up the possum.
To show a smile they have to frown,
Say those who've run across 'em.

Two Common Syllables

You know what a syllable in a word is.
It is a part of a word that has just one
vowel sound in it.

Read the sentences below. As you say
each word in heavy black letters, listen
for the number of syllables in it.

1. The man needed **help** with the box.
2. Sue had a **secret** friend that no one
   had ever seen.

How many vowel sounds do you hear
in help?

How many vowel sounds do you hear
in secret?

Now read the next two sentences.

3. My brother will stop and **play** with
   every **playful** dog he sees.
4. As the car came **near** the house, it **nearly**
   went over a big bump.

Look at the words in heavy black letters.
What letters were added to play to make
playful? How many vowel sounds do you hear
in play? How many vowel sounds do you hear
in playful? When ful was added to play,
a syllable was added.

What letters were added to near to make
nearly? How many vowel sounds do you hear
in near? How many vowel sounds do you hear
in nearly? When ly was added to near,
a syllable was added.

Say the words <u>playful</u> and <u>nearly</u>
to yourself and listen for the sounds
the letters <u>ful</u> and <u>ly</u> stand for. When you
come to word that ends with <u>ful</u> or <u>ly</u>,
think the right sounds for those letters.
That will help you in your reading.

Often a syllable is added to a word
to make another word. Syllables like
<u>ful</u> and <u>ly</u> are sometimes called **common
syllables.** You will often see them
added to words you know very well.

Read the sentences below. Use what
you know about common syllables to help
you read the words in heavy black letters.

5. Ted held **tightly** to his little brother's
   hand on the busy street.

6. We were all **thankful** that it turned out
   to be a nice day for the game.

7. Mom thanked Ed for being so **helpful**
   when Aunt Jane came to dinner.

8. When the new girl came to school, Ann
   secretly hoped she would be her friend.

9. The mouse went by the sleeping cat
   as **quietly** as it could.

10. Everyone was **hopeful** that the bird
    that had been hurt would get better.

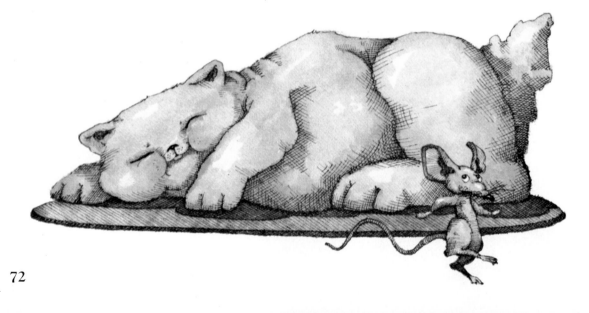

Clarence and the Burglar

by PATRICIA LAUBER

My name is Pat Logan. My brother's name
is Brian. And we have a dog named Clarence.

Almost everybody on our street likes Clarence
because he's so friendly. He doesn't growl
at anybody.

"Some watchdog!" George Harris would say.
George lives next door. He has a great big dog
named Wolf.

George would make fun of Clarence
because Clarence never growled at anybody.

"He's too friendly," George would say.
"He'll never make a watchdog."

But Clarence would just wag his tail.

Well, Clarence may not be much of a watchdog,
but he does like to play. If you don't play
with him, Clarence goes for your shoelace.
He pulls at the shoelace to get you to play
with him.

Clarence likes to watch TV, too. Every time
our TV is on, Clarence watches with Brian
and me.

He'll watch anything we watch. But he likes
ball games best of all.

Mom put an old chair in front of the TV,
just for Clarence. Now he knows that's
his chair. And that's where he sits when
he's watching TV.

Sometimes when all of us are out, Clarence
goes next door to visit Mr. and Mrs. Brundage.
They always let him in. Then Clarence sits
in front of their TV and watches the ball game
with them.

When the game is over, Clarence gets up
and goes home.

"That's some dog," the Brundages
always say.

And Clarence just wags his tail.

One night Mom and Brian and I went out
to visit some friends. We left Clarence
in the back yard.

There was a night game on TV.
So Clarence went next door to watch it
with Mr. and Mrs. Brundage.

While our house was dark, a burglar came.
He got into the house through a window.
He put some of our things into a bag.

The ball game on TV must have ended
just then, because Clarence came home
from the Brundages'. He came in
through the window the burglar had left open.

Inside he stopped. He smelled something.
A new friend! Someone to play with.

Clarence wagged his tail and jumped up
on the burglar. But the burglar didn't have
time to play.

So Clarence pulled first one shoelace
and then another. The burglar's shoelaces
came untied.

That's when we came home. Just as we got
to the house, we heard a terrible noise.

We ran in and put on the lights. There
was the burglar, out cold on the floor!
The bag with our things in it was beside him.
And so was Clarence, wagging his tail.

Mom called the police.

"Clarence must have wanted the burglar
to play with him," I said.

"Then he untied the burglar's shoelaces,"
said Brian.

"And that made the burglar trip and fall,"
said Mom.

"And now he's out like a light!" said Brian.

Just then George Harris came
to our front door. Wolf was with him.

"A burglar got into our house tonight,"
said George. "Wolf was asleep, or he would
have got him."

"Some watchdog," said Brian. "The burglar
is right here, out cold on the floor. He came
to our house, too. But our watchdog Clarence
was too much for him. Right, Clarence?"

And Clarence just wagged his tail.

Books to Enjoy

The Case of the Cat's Meow by Crosby Bonsall
Three boys help a friend to find his lost cat.
They get a big surprise.

What's Inside the Box?
by Ethel and Leonard Kessler
All the animals think a monster is in the box.
They don't find out for sure until the very end.

Ginger's Upstairs Pet by John Ryckman
When a tall animal comes to her house,
a little girl feeds it in a new way.

The Dog Who Came to Dinner
by Sydney Taylor
New friends come to dinner. To everyone's
surprise, a big dog comes to dinner, too!

Sea Frog, City Frog by Dorothy Van Woerkom
In this old Japanese story, two frogs want to go
to new places and see new things.

Skylights

MAGAZINE TWO

Contents

Good Lemonade

by FRANK ASCH

One summer Hank decided to have
a lemonade stand.

On the first day, Hank sold lemonade
to many of his friends. But by the next day,
the word was out. Hank's lemonade was
just terrible. All Hank sold was
one glass of lemonade — and that
was to his little brother.

"A lemonade stand is a good idea,"
said his friend Howie. "All you need now
is some *good* lemonade."

"What do you mean?" asked Hank.
"My lemonade is good enough. All I need
are some good signs."

So Hank made some signs. Soon there were signs for Hank's stand just about everywhere. Hank sat down and waited. But all he sold was one glass of lemonade — and that was to his little brother.

"Well," thought Hank, "that idea didn't work."

KEEP COOL
with
Hank's
Lemonade

Beat
the
Heat
with
Hank's
Lemonade

Join the parade
to Hank's Lemonade

Lemonade

So Hank painted his stand bright yellow.
And he decided to give away a prize
with every glass of lemonade. But all Hank
sold was one glass of lemonade — and that
was to his little brother.

"I need something that will make people really want to buy my lemonade," thought Hank.

So he got all dressed up as a big, bright yellow lemon. Hank looked really funny. But all he sold was one glass of lemonade — and that was to his little brother.

KEEP COOL
with
Hank's
Lemonade

Join the parade
Hank's Lemo...

Beat
the
Heat
with Hank's
Lemonade

Lemonade

Beat
the
Heat
with Hank's
Lemonade

The next day Hank sat all alone at his
lemonade stand, thinking of new ideas.
He saw a lot of people coming
down the street. Hank went after them
to see where they were going.

They all went right to Howie's
Lemonade Stand!

"What's your secret?" Hank asked Howie.

"*Good* lemonade," said Howie.

"I'll try anything once," thought Hank.

So he went home and made some more lemonade. But this time he made sure that it was *good* lemonade.

And it must have been *very* good lemonade. Hank sold every glass but one — the one he gave to his little brother.

What Could You Be?

What could you be when you grow up?
You can choose from so many things. Think
about the things you like to do now.

Do you have a garden? When you grow up,
you might work in a greenhouse.

Maybe you would like to grow plants
that people eat. Or you might take care of
trees and plants in a park.

Do you like sports? There are some sports you could play when you grow up. Or you could talk about other people who play.

You might work in a store like this. You would sell things people need for sports.

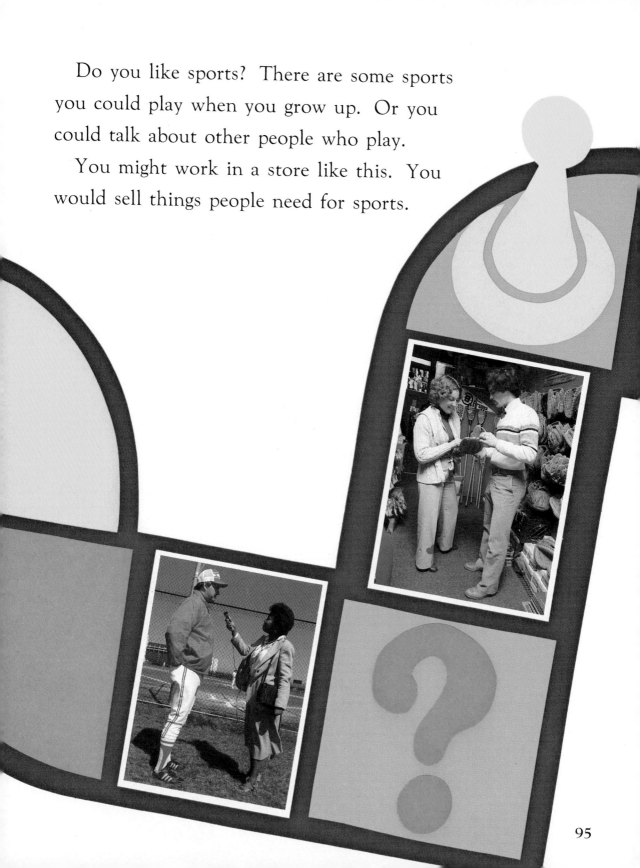

Do you like to find out what makes
things go?
You might work indoors
or outdoors
high up
or underground.

Maybe you like animals. Here are two ways you could work with them.

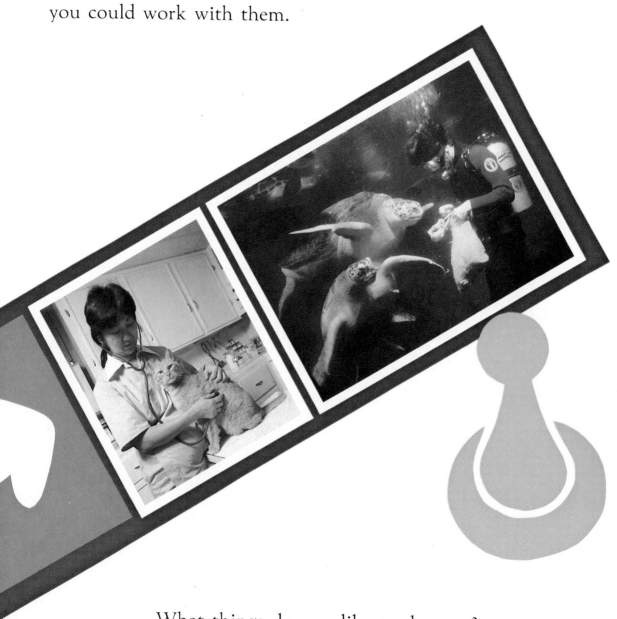

What things do you like to do now? They may help you to choose what you will be someday.

I Love Gram

by RUTH A. SONNEBORN

For Ellie, there was always Gram. It was Gram who was watching for Ellie when she got home from school. It was Gram who sat with her while she had her after-school snack. It was Gram who played with her and let her help get dinner ready.

When Mom came home from work, she was tired. And Ellie's big sister Lily always had homework to do.

But Gram was always there.

Then one day Mom sat down and talked
with Ellie. "Gram is sick," said Mom.
"She's in the hospital."

Gram sick? Gram was never sick!

"I don't want Gram to be sick!"
Ellie cried. "I don't want her to be
in the hospital. I want Gram to be home."

"I know. I know," Mom said. "Lily and I
want her home, too, and she will be soon."
She hugged Ellie.

"While Gram is in the hospital, you will
go home with Joey after school. You'll stay
at his house until Lily comes to get you."

At dinner that night, everyone was quiet.
Ellie didn't like looking at Gram's
empty chair. And in bed that night, Ellie
could not fall asleep.

Mom came in. "I know you miss Gram,"
she said. She sat on the bed next to Ellie.
Soon Ellie went to sleep.

The next morning at breakfast, Ellie looked very sad.

"Don't look so sad, Ellie," Mom said. "Gram will be well soon."

After school that day, Ellie went home with Joey.

The days went by. Every day Ellie went home
with Joey. Every night she helped Lily
get dinner ready. And every night she asked,
"Mom, is Gram coming home tomorrow?"

Mom always shook her head. "Not tomorrow,
but soon."

"Soon, soon, soon," thought Ellie. "How long
do I have to wait for *soon* to be *now*?"

Then one morning Mom was up early.
She was smiling. "I have some good news,"
she said.

"Gram!" Ellie said. "Is Gram coming home?"

"Yes," Mom said. "Gram is coming home
tomorrow. I will stop by for her
at the hospital. Tomorrow night we will
all have dinner together."

Ellie began to dance around the room.
"My Gram is coming home tomorrow,"
she sang over and over.

In school Ellie told her teacher
the good news. "I'm making a surprise
for Gram," she said.

She showed her teacher the picture
she had made. It was a picture of a girl
and a woman. "That's me. And see,"
she said, "this woman is Gram."

Coming Home

The next day after school, Joey and Ellie played outside. They began to play hide-and-seek. While Ellie was waiting for Joey to hide, she had an idea.

"Maybe," she thought, "Gram is home already. Why should I wait for Lily? I know the way home."

She didn't say a word to Joey. She just ran off. And soon she was right in front of her house. She ran up the steps as fast as she could. She tried the front door. The door would not open.

"Gram," Ellie called. "Gram, are you there?" There was no answer.

Then Ellie pounded on the door. "Gram! Lily! Mom! Gram!" she called.

But no one answered.

Meanwhile, Joey got tired of waiting
to be found. He came out of his hiding place.

"It's not your turn to hide, Ellie!"
he shouted. "It's *my* turn."

He looked everywhere he could think of.
But he could not find Ellie. He went inside
to tell his mother.

Joey's mother said, "Maybe Lily came
for her early. Maybe they forgot to tell
you they were going. I'll call her house."

No one answered.

Joey's mother was just getting ready
to look for Ellie outside again when
Lily came. "Ellie must have gone home
by herself," Lily said. "I'll run and see."

Lily ran home as fast as she could.
And there was Ellie sitting on the top step.
Lily was happy to see her, but she asked,
"Why didn't you wait for me?"

Ellie said, "I thought Gram would
be home already. I want to see her."

"You knew Gram was coming home
with Mom," said Lily. "That means she won't
get home until dinnertime. Come on,
let's go in and get dinner ready."

They went inside. Lily told Ellie to call
Joey's mother so she wouldn't worry anymore.
Then while Lily began to get dinner, Ellie
put up her surprise.

"See," she told Lily, "I'm putting my picture
where Gram can look at it while she's eating."

Lily asked Ellie to set the table.
Lily said, "Try to make the table look pretty
for Gram."

Ellie liked the idea. When the table was
all set, Ellie said, "Now, *that* looks pretty."

Then she went over to the window.
"I'm going to watch for Mom's car," she said.

Ellie watched many cars go down the street.
After a while she shouted, "Lily, Lily!
Mom and Gram are here!"

Ellie ran to open the door. She gave Gram
a great big hug.

"I missed you, Gram," she said.

"And I missed you, too," said Gram.

Then they went inside together.

At Mrs. Appleby's

by ELIZABETH UPHAM McWEBB

When frost is shining on the trees,
   It's spring at Mrs. Appleby's.
You smell it in the air before
   You step inside the kitchen door.

Rows of scarlet flowers bloom
   From every window in the room.
And funny little speckled fish
   Are swimming in a china dish.

A tiny bird with yellow wings
   Just sits and sings and sings and SINGS!
Outside when frost is on the trees,
   It's spring at Mrs. Appleby's.

Getting Help from Commas

Often in your reading you will see a comma like this , after a word. Commas can help to make the meaning of a sentence clear. One way a comma can help is by showing you who is being spoken to. Read this sentence:

1. Hank, I hear you gave some lemonade to your brother.

The person spoken to in this sentence is Hank. The word <u>Hank</u> is followed by a comma to show that Hank is being spoken to. What did you do when you came to the comma? You should have made a little pause.

Now read these two sentences:

2. Lydia has time to help Dr. Arnold.
3. Lydia has time to help, Dr. Arnold.

In which of those two sentences is Dr. Arnold being spoken to? How could you tell that? The comma helped you.

Every little comma helps. Use some today!

Commas can help in another way, too.
Read this sentence:

4. Mrs. Parker said she'd help us.

Do you know who Mrs. Parker is?
The sentence does not tell you much about her.
Now read this:

5. Mrs. Parker, the sign painter next door,
said she'd help us.

Now you do know who Mrs. Parker is.
What helped you to know that? The words
between the commas helped you to know that.
Sometimes you see commas before and
after a group of words. These words tell
something more about someone or something
that has just been named.

Now read these sentences. You will see how the commas help make the meaning clear.

6. Susie, my sister's cat, is not happy about having to move.
7. I gave the book to Mr. Moss, my brother's teacher, when I came in.
8. Dr. Gold, Ellie's mother, is a friend of my mother's.

The two sentences below have the same words but do not have commas in the same places. Use what you know about commas to help you understand the meaning of each sentence.

9. Teddy, my friend from school was home sick today.
10. Teddy, my friend from school, was home sick today.

Which sentence tells who Teddy is? Which sentence tells that Teddy is the one being spoken to?

Read the following pairs of sentences that use the same words but do not have commas in the same places. The commas will help make the meaning of each sentence clear.

11. Betty, my older sister, is making a tree house.

12. Betty, my older sister is making a tree house.

13. Jess, the boy next door asked us to come over to his house.

14. Jess, the boy next door, asked us to come over to his house.

Impossible, Possum

by ELLEN CONFORD

Randolph was a little possum. His mother
worried about him.

"I don't understand it," she said.
"All possums hang by their tails and sleep
upside down. Why can't you?"

"I don't know," Randolph said sadly.
"I try hard enough."

"Try again," said his father. "Maybe you just need more practice."

"All right," said Randolph. He walked out onto a branch of their tree.

"Don't look down," said his father.

"Don't be scared," said his mother.

"You can do it!" called his brother Eugene.

"No, he can't," said his sister Geraldine.

Randolph curled his tail around the branch. When he let go with his paws, he was hanging by his tail.

"Good for you!" shouted his father.

"You're doing it!" shouted his brother.

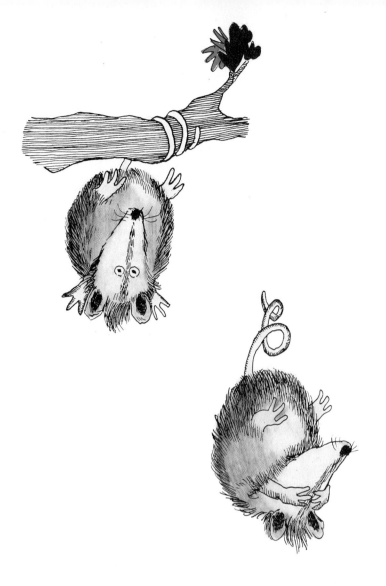

"No, he's not," said his sister
as Randolph's tail uncurled. Randolph fell
to the ground, head first.

"Oh, my!" said his mother. They all ran
to help Randolph.

"Are you hurt?" asked his mother.

"No more than any other time," said Randolph.

"I just don't understand it," said his father.
"Your mother and I can hang by our tails.
Your sister Geraldine can hang by her tail.
Possums always sleep upside down.

"Why don't you try it again?" his father said.
"You almost had it last time."

"It's just impossible," Randolph answered.
"I just can't do it."

"Yes, you can," said his mother.
"You just have to keep trying."

"I *can't* keep trying!" cried Randolph.
"Every time I try, I fall on my head."

"If you didn't hurt your head all the time,
would you keep trying?" asked Eugene.

"I guess so," said Randolph. "But how
could I keep from hurting my head?"

"We could put a big pile of leaves
under the tree," Eugene said. "Then if you fall,
you won't get hurt."

"*If* he falls! You mean, *when* he falls,"
said Geraldine.

"That's enough, Geraldine," said her father.
"It's a very good idea. Now, go help
your brothers get some leaves."

Randolph, Eugene, and Geraldine ran around
getting leaves. They made a big pile of them
under the branch where Randolph practiced.

"Here I go again," said Randolph. He climbed
up the tree and out onto the branch. He curled
his tail over the branch and hung upside down.
His tail uncurled, and he fell head first
into the pile of leaves.

"Do the leaves help?" asked his mother.

"A little," said Randolph as he climbed
up the tree once more.

Again and again he tried to hang by his tail.
Again and again he fell onto the pile of leaves.

His brother and sister went off to play.
His mother went in to make dinner. His father
went for a walk.

Randolph kept hanging and falling.

At last he gave up.

"I have fallen for the last time," he said
to himself as he sat in the pile of leaves.

"Maybe other possums can sleep upside down,
but I am different. Let the others sleep
upside down on the branch. I will sleep
on my pile of leaves. It's really nice enough
here. I may even go to sleep right now."
And he did.

They're Stuck!

Randolph woke to find that Geraldine and
Eugene were jumping into his pile of leaves.

"Whee!" shouted Geraldine. "This is fun!"

"It may be fun for you," Randolph said sadly.
"For me, it's just a place to sleep."

He got up. Some leaves stuck to his tail.

"I'll help you," said Eugene. He tried
to take the leaves off Randolph's tail,
but they wouldn't come off.

"They're stuck on," he said.

"Don't be silly," said Geraldine. "How can
they be stuck?"

She pulled a leaf off Randolph's tail.

"Ouch!" said Randolph. "That hurts!"

"Look!" Geraldine said. "Sap is coming out of that small branch on the tree."

"Sap!" said Eugene. "You got sap on your tail. That's what made the leaves stick!"

Randolph stopped pulling leaves from his tail.

"Why didn't I think of this before?" he cried. He held his tail under the branch.

"Sap makes leaves stick to my tail," Randolph shouted as he raced up the tree. "Maybe it will make my tail stick to the branch."

Randolph curled his tail around the branch. He held on with his paws until he was sure the sap was sticking. Then he let go and hung down. He didn't fall.

"Look at me!" he shouted. "Look, everyone!"

His mother came outside to look. His father heard the noise and came running.

"He's doing it!" Eugene cried. "Randolph's hanging by his tail!"

"Good for you, Randolph," said his father. "You see, you just needed some practice."

"I don't think it was the practice so much as the sap," Randolph said.

"Sap?" said his father.

"Sap?" said his mother.

"Sap," said Eugene. "Isn't that a good idea?"

"But how are you going to get down?" asked Geraldine.

"I never thought of that," Randolph said.

"Don't worry," his mother said. "We'll just uncurl your tail for you when you want to come down."

"Well, I think I'll just hang here for a while," said Randolph. "Everything is so different upside down."

He shut his eyes and fell asleep.

From then on, Randolph held his tail
under the sap before the possums went to sleep.
His mother would uncurl it for him
when he woke up.

But one day Randolph saw that the sap
had dried up.

"What will I do now?" he cried.

"Maybe you should try again without the sap,"
said his father.

"It's impossible," said Randolph.
"I always fall on my head."

"Randolph," said his father, "winter
is coming. In the winter, sap dries up.
You must try to hang like the others do."

"Maybe we can find another tree with the sap
coming out," said Eugene. "I'll help you look."

So Randolph and Eugene went off together
to look for some more sap.

"It's impossible," said Randolph
after they had been looking for some time.
"I guess Father was right."

Sadly, Randolph and Eugene walked
back home. "I might as well start making
another pile of leaves," said Randolph.
"I'll need a place to sleep."

Just then Geraldine came racing up.

"Look what I found!" she called. "I found
some sap, and I put it on these leaves,"
she said, smiling. "Would you like me
to put it on your tail?"

"That's very nice of you, Geraldine,"
said Randolph. He held out his tail.

Then he ran up the tree.

"I hope you put enough on," he worried.

"Oh, I did," said Geraldine happily.

His mother and father came out.

"Geraldine found some sap for me," Randolph said.

"What a good sister!" said his mother.

"It was nothing," said Geraldine.

"Look!" called Randolph, who was hanging by his tail. "It works! Thank you, Geraldine."

Geraldine cried, "Randolph, you're doing it! Look at Randolph! He's doing it!"

"Sure he's doing it," said Eugene. "He can always do it with the sap on his tail."

"No, no, no!" cried Geraldine, hopping
up and down. "It wasn't sap. It was water!
I put water on the leaves. It was a trick!"

"Water!" cried Randolph.

"What?" said his father.

"Oh, my," said his mother.

"That was a mean trick," said Eugene.

"But he *is* hanging by his tail!" Geraldine
said. "By *himself!*"

"I am?" cried Randolph.

"You are!" said his father.

"Oh, Randolph, I'm so happy for you!"
said his mother.

"I can do it! I can do it!" Randolph shouted.

"All you needed was to believe you could," said his father.

"And a tricky sister," said Eugene.

"You mean a helpful sister," said Geraldine.

The possums were so happy that they ran out onto the branch and sang "For He's a Jolly Good Fellow" to Randolph as he hung upside down by his tail.

And no one sang louder than Randolph.

More Potatoes

by MILLICENT E. SELSAM

One day Sue went to the store to get
potatoes for her mother. The storekeeper
sold her his last bag of potatoes.

"How will you get more?" asked Sue.

The storekeeper said he would get more
from the warehouse.

Very early the next morning, Sue went
to the store again. The warehouse truck
was there. On the sidewalk were boxes
and bags. Sue found some bags that
had the word POTATOES on them.

That day at school, Sue told her class
about buying the last bag of potatoes.
She told them about the truck that brought
more potatoes to the store.

The children wanted to know more
about where potatoes come from.
Mrs. Ling, their teacher, called Mr. Bartlett.
He had a potato farm not far away.
Mr. Bartlett said the class could come
to visit his farm.

On Tuesday, the class rode out to the farm.
Mr. Bartlett was waiting for them.

"The potatoes are already in the ground," said Mr. Bartlett.

"You mean we are too late?" asked Sue.

"No, but the potato plants are already growing. I planted them in May. Now it is June."

"Do you plant potatoes from seeds?" asked Mrs. Ling.

"No," said Mr. Bartlett. "We plant small potatoes. We call them *seed* potatoes." He took a seed potato from his pocket.

"Every piece of potato we plant must have one or more eyes. The eyes are the places on the potato where the buds come out. New potato plants grow from these buds."

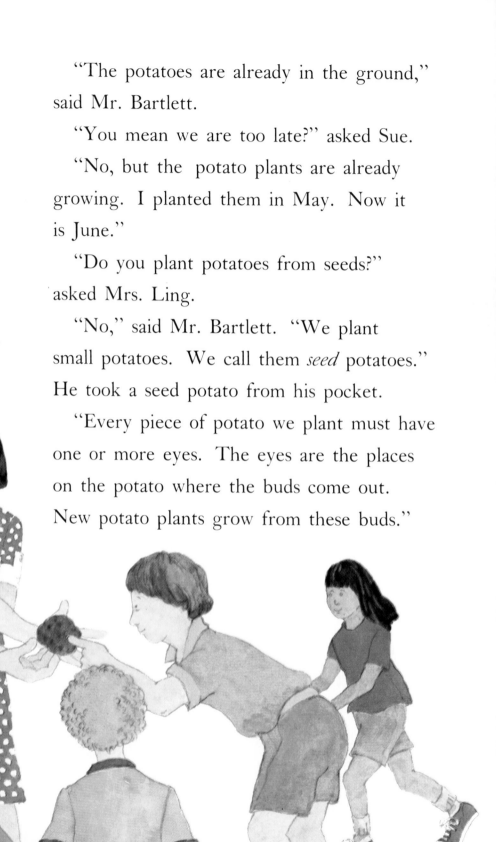

He cut the seed potato into four pieces.

"How do you plant the pieces?" asked one
of the boys. "Does someone go along
and plant them in the ground?"

"Oh, no," said Mr. Bartlett. "The farm is
too big for that. I have a machine that
plants the potatoes." He took the class
to show them the machine. "This machine
plants two rows of potatoes at a time.

"Do you want to see what the potato plants
look like now?" asked Mr. Bartlett.
"Follow me."

They followed Mr. Bartlett to the field.
As far as they could see, there were rows
of green plants. There were small
white flowers on the plants.

"I see the plants," said Sue. "But where
are the potatoes?"

Mr. Bartlett dug under one of the plants.
Then he took the plant out of the ground.
"Now find the potatoes," he said.

The children looked. The potatoes were small, but they were there. They were on the roots of the plant.

"They will grow bigger all through the summer," said Mr. Bartlett. "Look here. You will see the seed potato that we planted."

"Who will dig up the potatoes when they are ready?" asked one of the girls.

"A big machine will dig them up in September," said Mr. Bartlett.

"May we come then to see how the machine works?" asked Mrs. Ling.

"Yes," said Mr. Bartlett. "I'll let you know when the potatoes are ready to be dug up."

The Big Machine

In September, Sue went back to school.
Sue asked Mrs. Ling, "When can we go
to see Mr. Bartlett?"

"I already have a note from him,"
said Mrs. Ling. "We can visit his farm
next Wednesday."

On Wednesday, the class went back
to the farm. This time Mrs. Bartlett
was there, too.

There was a big truck in the field.
Beside it was a tractor. The tractor
was pulling a big machine.

One of the children said, "The potato plants
are all brown!"

"That is the way they *should* look
when we dig them," said Mr. Bartlett.
"When the tops turn brown, we know
the potatoes under the ground are ready.
Please move away from the machines now."

The children moved back. Mr. Bartlett started the tractor that pulled the big digging machine. Mrs. Bartlett started the truck that went along beside it.

The machine dug two rows of potatoes
at a time. Potatoes started going
up a moving belt on the machine.
Dirt and vines fell through to the ground.
But the potatoes stayed on the belt
and went on into the truck.

After a while Mrs. Bartlett stopped the truck,
and Mr. Bartlett stopped the tractor. "Here,"
he said to the children. "You may each have
a potato to take back to school."

Laugh Lines

Ron: Where are you going
with the watering can?
Don: To water the flowers.
Ron: But it's raining now!
Don: That's all right.
I have my raincoat on.

Why does
your dog
keep turning
around and
around?

He's a
watchdog and
he's winding
himself up.

Take Two

What two words
are all tied up?

shoe + *lace* =
shoelace

What two words are always
getting stepped on?

side + *walk* =
sidewalk

What two words
are all wet?

under + *water* =
underwater

The Secret Hiding Place

by RAINEY BENNETT

Little Hippo was the pet of all the hippos.
Every morning the big hippos waited for him
to get up so they could take care of him.

"Sh-Sh," they whispered. "Little Hippo
is sleeping."

Every morning the big hippos would get
breakfast for Little Hippo. Then they
all sat down to watch Little Hippo eat.
One morning Little Hippo felt cross.
"I don't want any breakfast," he said. "I wish
the hippos wouldn't watch everything I do.
I wish I could be by myself once in a while."
"Don't eat so fast," Big Charles said.

All the hippos went along when Big Charles
took Little Hippo for his morning walk.

"We will take care of you," said Big Charles.

But Little Hippo didn't want all the hippos
to come. He wanted to go looking around
by himself. What fun is a walk
with nineteen hippos?

Without even saying, "Please, may I,"
Little Hippo ran to some bushes.

"Stop, Little Hippo," Big Charles shouted.
"Birds nest there."

"Don't go in the tall grass where
zebras hide. Do you want to get stripes?"

Little Hippo stopped to look at an ostrich that was hiding its head.

"Come away, Little Hippo," Big Charles shouted. "He thinks he's hiding."

When Big Charles got to Little Hippo, he was
hot and cross. "That's a chameleon's house.
Come away right now!" he puffed.

"Don't you know better than to go looking
into secret places?" Big Charles asked.

Everyone in the forest had a hiding place it seemed — everyone but Little Hippo. The tiger had a place in the tall grass. Monkeys went up in trees. Even the elephant could hide. He was nearly hidden by leaves as big as his ears.

"You're lucky," Little Hippo told the turtle.
"You have your hiding place with you. What's
it like inside?"

"It's dark," said the turtle.

What Kind of Place?

Little Hippo was still cross at lunch.
But later that day, after he'd had some sleep,
there was a big surprise.

"We will play hide-and-seek," Big Charles
said. "I will be IT." Standing by a tree,
he started to count. "I will count
to one hundred," said Big Charles.

"Now!" Little Hippo whispered. "Now I can
find a hiding place of my very own."

He ran to the flowering trees.

"Little Hippo, Little Hippo, come hide
with us," some hippos called.

But Little Hippo wanted his own
hiding place. "I'll hide in the river,"
he thought.

"Little Hippo, Little Hippo, hide with us,"
some other hippos cried.

"Oh, no," Little Hippo said to himself.

The lion laughed when he saw Little Hippo
trying to hide under a rock.

"Silly hippo," he said. "That's no place
to hide. Follow me. You can hide in my cave."

163

"Are we almost there?" asked Little Hippo.

"Here we are," said the lion. "Make yourself at home."

Then he went off to look for something to eat and left Little Hippo all alone.

The dark cave was full of funny noises.

"I'm scared," said Little Hippo. "I don't want to be alone *this* much."

Little Hippo was so scared that he ran out of the cave.

He ran for a long, long time. At last he stopped running.

"I can't run anymore," he puffed.

Just then the chameleon put its head out of its house.

"Why, hello, Little Hippo," he said. "What are you doing here?"

"I'm lost," said Little Hippo.

"You're lost?" said the chameleon. "Follow me!"

He took Little Hippo to the top of a small hill.

"Now look down, Little Hippo!"

And there right below him was Big Charles.
He and all the other hippos were looking
for something. "Little Hippo, come out,"
they called, pushing through the grass.

"Come out, come out wherever you are!"
they shouted, looking under rocks.

But not one of them thought of looking up.

Little Hippo laughed and laughed. "They'll
never find me here," he said. "They don't see
me, and I'm right up here."

"Home free, home free," Little Hippo shouted
as he ran up to Big Charles.

All the big hippos were so happy to see him!
They shouted and stamped their feet.

"Where did you hide, Little Hippo? We looked
everywhere," said Big Charles.

But Little Hippo didn't tell him. He just
smiled, because he knew that the big hippos
would always look everywhere but up. And he
never told anyone about his secret hiding place
where he could be alone, but not too alone.

Using the Alphabet

If someone asked you to count, you would not have any trouble. You would start with the numbers 1, 2, 3, 4 and go on. You know the order of numbers, so you can count.

Knowing the order of numbers can help you find things.

Letters can be in order, too. When letters are in order, we call that the **alphabet.**

A B C D E F G H I J K L M
N O P Q R S T U V W X Y Z

The alphabet can also help you to find things. Have you ever tried to look for someone's name in a telephone book? If you have, you know that all the last names in a telephone book are in the order of the alphabet. We say that they are in **alphabetical order.**

Let's look at some first names that are in alphabetical order.

The name <u>Ann</u> is first because <u>A</u> is the first letter of the alphabet. The name <u>Bob</u> is next because <u>B</u> is the next letter of the alphabet. Why is the name <u>Carol</u> next? Why is the name <u>David</u> last?

These names are not in alphabetical order. Now let's put them in order.

Do any of these names begin with A? Do any of these names begin with B? Do any of these names begin with C? Yes, Carla does. The first name should be Carla.

What letter comes after C in the alphabet? Do any of the names begin with that letter? What letter comes after D? Do any of the names begin with that letter? Yes, Eric begins with an E. The name Eric should come next.

Which name should come next, Lisa or Tony? Why? That's right. The name Lisa would come next because the letter L comes before the letter T in the alphabet.

Escalators

by CANDICE TAYLOR

Escalators are nervous stairs
That simply can't hold still,
But think how handy they would be
For climbing up a hill!

The House That Nobody Wanted

by LILIAN MOORE

There was once an old house that stood
on a hill. It had gray doors, gray windows,
and gray walls.

An old man and an old woman lived
in this house. And they had lived there
for a long time.

The old man and the old woman did not
go out very much. But one day they went
to visit some friends.

They got into their car and rode away.
They rode uphill and downhill and then
uphill and downhill again.

At last they saw the house of their friends.
It was a little red house with white doors
and windows. All around the house, flowers
and green plants grew in the sun.

The old man and the old woman had
a good time with their friends. Then they
got back into their car and went home.

They rode uphill and downhill,
then uphill and downhill again.

At last they came to their house.

"My!" said the old woman. "Our house
is *very* gray, isn't it?"

"And there is nothing green to see when
we look out," said the old man.

"Let's sell this house!" said the old woman.
"Then we can buy a pretty house!"

" . . . with grass and flowers around it!"
said the old man.

So the old man and the old woman tried
to sell their house.

First a man came to look at it.

"No," he said. "This house is too gray
for me. I like a red house."

And he went away.

"Let's paint the house red," said the
old man. "Then maybe the next one
will buy it."

So the old man and the old woman painted
the house red.

Soon after, a woman came to look
at the house.

"I like a house that has white windows
and white doors," she said. And she
went away.

So the old man and the old woman painted
the windows white. They painted the doors
white, too.

Soon after that, a man and a woman came
to see the house. They liked the outside.

"But it is so gray inside," said the woman.

And they went away.

So this time the old man and
the old woman painted the walls inside
the house. They painted some walls
yellow and some walls blue.

Soon another man came to see the house.

"This is a pretty house," he said. "But I
am looking for a home with a garden."

And he, too, went away.

The old man and the old woman began
to work on a garden.

Soon green plants began to grow in the sun.

Then one day there were flowers — red
and blue and yellow — growing all around
the house.

"Now," said the old woman, "someone
will want to buy this house! Then at last
we can buy the house *we* want."

The man looked around.

"What kind of a house *do* we want?" he asked.

"We want a pretty house," said the old woman.

"Painted inside and out?" asked the old man.

"Oh yes!" answered the old woman.

"With grass and flowers growing around it?" asked the old man.

"Oh yes!" she answered again.

The old man laughed.

"Look around you," he told her.

So the old woman looked around.

She saw a red house with white windows and doors.

Inside the house she saw bright yellow and blue walls.

Outside she saw grass and a garden
with flowers growing in the sun.

"Oh my!" she said in surprise. "This is
a pretty house, isn't it?"

"This is just the house we want!"
said the old man.

So the old man and the old woman went
right on living in their house on the hill.

A Window

by DAVID BEARS HEART

A window:
a place to look
and see the beautiful trees,
a place for wind and air to
come and go as they please.
Most of all a window is
a picture hanging on my wall.

Books to Enjoy

Grandma Is Somebody Special
by Susan Goldman
   A little girl likes the stories her grandmother
tells and the nice things she does.

Socks for Supper by Jack Kent
   An old woman finds a new way to get something
to eat.

George and Martha by James Marshall
   Here are stories about two hippos who are
the best of friends.

Papa's Lemonade by Eve Rice
   How Papa makes lemonade without lemons is one
of the funny stories in this book.

Baseball Brothers by Jeff Rubin and Rick Rael
   Two boys want to go to a big ball game and meet
one of the best players.

Skylights

MAGAZINE THREE

Contents

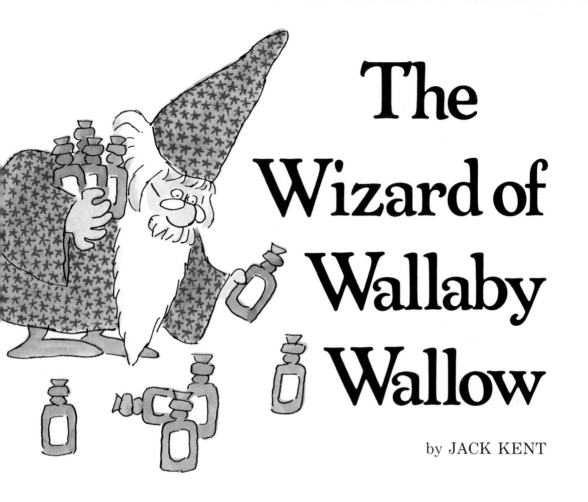

The Wizard of Wallaby Wallow

by JACK KENT

The Wizard of Wallaby Wallow
had spells for turning people
into everything from A to Z.

Every spell was in a little bottle.

Every bottle had a label that told
what kind of spell it was.

But the bottles were all out of order.
The wizard could never find the bottle
he wanted.

So now the wizard was very busy.
He was trying to get all his magic spells
in order. He had taken down all the bottles.
Now he was carefully putting the spells
back up in order.

"I wonder what kind of spell *this* is," said
the wizard. He was looking at the bottle
in his hand. "The label has come off."

Just then he heard someone at the door.

"Oh, no!" cried the wizard. "I'm never left
alone long enough to get anything finished."

He opened the door and said, "Go away.
I'm busy. SHOO!"

But the visitor was a mouse. He was used
to having people shout "shoo" at him. So he
didn't much care what the wizard said to him.

"I want to buy a magic spell,"
the mouse said. "I'm tired of being
a mouse. I want to be something else."

"Like what?" asked the wizard.

"I haven't decided," said the mouse. "I thought I'd come and see what kinds of spells you had."

"Everything is out of order right now," said the wizard. "Come back tomorrow and . . .

"Wait a minute!" he said. He looked at the bottle in his hand. "Here. You can have this one. It's free." And he handed the bottle to the mouse.

"There isn't any label on it," said the mouse. "What will it turn me into?"

"Something else," said the wizard. "That's
what you said you wanted to be!" Then
he shut the door and went back to putting
his spells in order.

The mouse went home and set the bottle on the table. Then he tried to guess what the magic spell would turn him into.

A butterfly, maybe? Butterflies are pretty. But they don't live very long. He would just as soon not be a butterfly.

Turtles live a long time. But they are so slow. The mouse hoped he wouldn't turn into a turtle.

A bee, maybe? Bees are fast, but they work very hard. Work was *not* one of the things the mouse most liked to do.

"What if I turned into a cat!" the mouse thought. "Cats eat mice!" He turned white at the thought.

"Now, I might turn into an elephant,"
thought the mouse. "But an elephant couldn't
get into my house."

The mouse couldn't think of anything
the spell might turn him into that would
make him happy.

"Being me has its problems," he decided.
"But I *do* know what they are. Whatever
I turn into might have bigger problems."

So he took the magic spell back
to the wizard.

The wizard wasn't too pleased when he had
to go to the door again. He was still upset
from putting the bottles in order. At first
he didn't remember who the mouse was.

Then he said, "You've changed."

"I may have," said the mouse. "Remember,
I wasn't a very happy mouse before. And now
I'm ... well ... something else."

"Was it the magic spell that changed you?"
asked the wizard.

"I guess it was," said the mouse.

"Then that's the first time one of
my spells ever worked!" said the wizard.
He was very pleased.

"It looks as if it worked two times,"
said the mouse. "It made us *both* happy.
It's a wonderful magic spell!"

The wizard went into his shop. He took
the labels off *all* the bottles. Then he put
the bottles back any old way.

Putting them in order was no longer
a problem.

Caterpillars

by AILEEN FISHER

What do caterpillars do?
Nothing much but chew and chew.

What do caterpillars know?
Nothing much but how to grow.

They just eat what by and by
will make them be a butterfly.

But that is more than I can do
however much I chew and chew.

201

Finding Clues

The sentences below are about a girl named Karen. You will find some clues in them to help you decide what Karen is doing.

Karen was alone in her room. She was all dressed up. She held up a tall black hat. The hat looked empty. Then she waved her hand over the hat and said some funny words. Karen put her hand into the hat. When she pulled her hand out, there was a rabbit in it!

"That was good, Peter," she said to her pet rabbit. "I hope it works that well tomorrow in school."

Which of these sentences is true?

1. Karen did not know the rabbit was
   in her hat.
2. Karen was practicing for a show
   at school the next day.
3. Karen's pet rabbit surprised her
   by jumping out of a hat.

How did you know the answer?
The sentences told you only a little
about what Karen was doing. But they did
give you some other clues about her. Here
is one of them.

She held up a tall black hat.

Did you find any others?

The sentences that follow tell something
that happened to a boy named Dan. Read
them and answer the question that follows.

Dan jumped out of bed and ran
to the window.

"Oh, oh," he said. "It's already late."

He got dressed as fast as he could.
Then he found his basketball and
raced out the back door.

When he got to the park, the others
were already there.

"Good," said Fran. "Now we can play."

Which of these sentences is true?

1. Dan was late for school.
2. Dan was going to a race
   in the park.
3. Dan was going to play ball
   with some other children.

What clues helped you answer
the question?

Choosing

by ELEANOR FARJEON

Which will you have, a ball or a cake?
A cake is so nice, yes, that's what I'll take.

Which will you have, a cake or a cat?
A cat is so soft, I think I'll take that.

Which will you have, a cat or a rose?
A rose is so sweet, I'll have that, I suppose.

Which will you have, a rose or a book?
A book full of pictures? — oh, do let me look!

Which will you have, a book or a ball?
Oh, a ball! No, a book; No, a —
   There! have them all!

Amy for Short

by LAURA JOFFE NUMEROFF

My name is Amelia Ann Sue Lee Brandon.
Amy for short. But I'm tall.

I'm the tallest girl in my class.

Mark is as tall as I am. He's my best friend.
He lives on the same street as I do. He has
a frog named Fred and a cat named Harriet.

Last summer Mark and I wanted to buy
a ring. It was a Secret Code Ring.

We were going to send away for it. So we
were trying to save up to get it. We hadn't
saved enough by the time I went to camp.

I was the tallest girl at camp. I signed up
for painting, swimming, and boating.

I wrote letters to Mark. He answered
my letters, but sometimes I couldn't read what
he wrote. It would have been nice to have had
a Secret Code Ring then.

Two things were different when I got home
from camp. My turtle Howie was bigger.
And I was an inch taller than Mark.

Every two minutes Mark would say,
"Let's measure again." We must have
measured a hundred times.

I was afraid Mark wasn't going to be
my best friend anymore, just because I was
an inch taller than he was.

My birthday was coming up soon. My mother
said I could have a party.

I asked ten of my friends. I sent notes
to all of them.

All of my friends called to say they
were coming — all but Mark. I was sure
he didn't want to be my best friend anymore.

So I called Mark. He said he couldn't come
because he had to play in a ball game
against Waynie Phillips. He wanted to beat
Waynie Phillips. Waynie Phillips is
the biggest boy on our street.

What fun is a birthday party without
your best friend? I asked my mother
if we could forget about the party.

"Amy, what would you tell your friends
who *are* coming?" asked Mother.

"I could say I wasn't having a party
this year," I said.

"I think it's too late to change it now, Amy.
Don't worry about Mark."

But I did worry — a lot.

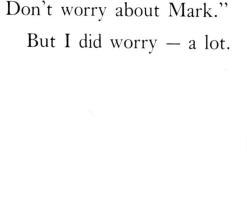

On the day of my party, I felt sad.

While we were eating breakfast, someone came
to the door. I thought it might be Mrs. Lowry
with my birthday cake. We had ordered
a white cake with red flowers on it.

I opened the door, but no one was there.
I looked all around. On the top step was a box
with a note on it.

The note was in code.

I pulled off the paper and opened the box.
In the box was another box!

I opened that box. In it there was a ball
of paper tied with string. I untied the string.
I took out still another box.

I opened that box — and there was
a Secret Code Ring! I ran inside.
I couldn't wait to read the message.

I got a piece of paper and a pencil. I held
the ring while my mother called off the numbers
from the note. I found the numbers on my ring
and wrote down the letters. Soon we had
the message.

It said:

If it is not too
late, can I still
come to your
party? I can
beat Waynie
Phillips any old
time. Mark

Codes
and Secret
Messages

AFUP KH
QRPGT
DEKH DTGG.

2-12-6 23-18-23
18-7 9-18-20-19-7.

Can you read these messages? Each message
is written in a different code. Whoever
wrote the message had a copy of the code.
Whoever wants to *read* the message will need
a copy of the code, too.

There are many different kinds of codes
you can use to write secret messages.
The next pages tell about some of them.

Number Codes

In some codes, a different number is used
for each letter. Here is one number code:

A=26   H=19   N=13   T=7
B=25   I=18   O=12   U=6
C=24   J=17   P=11   V=5
D=23   K=16   Q=10   W=4
E=22   L=15   R=9   X=3
F=21   M=14   S=8   Y=2
G=20   Z=1

Can you read this message now?

2-12-6   23-18-23
18-7   9-18-20-19-7.

You can make up your own number code.
Be sure to use a different number for
each letter.

Letter Codes

In letter codes, one letter is used to stand for another letter. Here is one way to make a letter code:

A=I	H=E	N=R	T=D
B=J	I=K	O=F	U=Q
C=S	J=M	P=Z	V=X
D=P	K=B	Q=Y	W=O
E=G	L=U	R=T	X=C
F=L	M=N	S=H	Y=W
G=A			Z=V

Can you read the message on the tree?

AFUP KH
QRPGT
DEKH DTGG.

Picture Codes

Here is a picture code. In a picture code, a different picture is used for each letter.

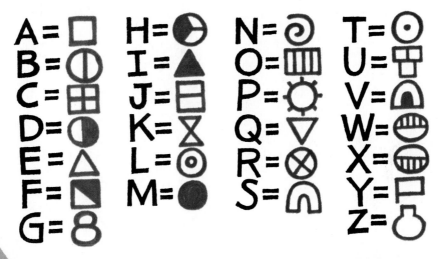

Can you read this now?

Here are the things you should do when you want to send a secret message:

1. Make up your own code or use one you just read about.

2. Use the code when you write out your secret message.

3. Give the message and a copy of the code to your friend.

The Folk Who Live in Backward Town

by MARY ANN HOBERMAN

The folk who live in Backward Town
Are inside out and upside down.
They wear their hats inside their heads
And go to sleep beneath their beds.
They only eat the apple peeling
And take their walks across the ceiling.

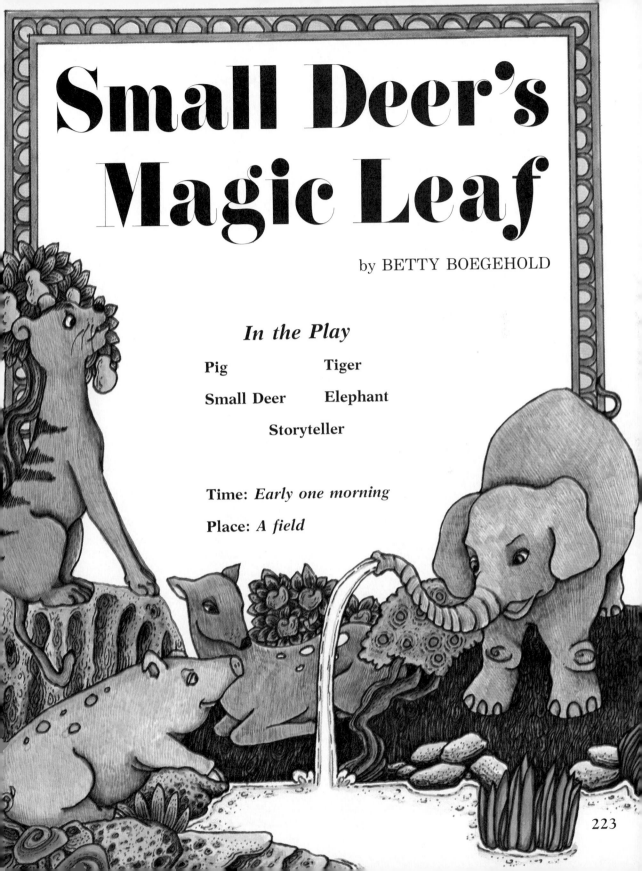

Small Deer's Magic Leaf

by BETTY BOEGEHOLD

In the Play

Pig   Tiger

Small Deer   Elephant

Storyteller

Time: *Early one morning*

Place: *A field*

Storyteller: One morning Small Deer was out playing when she fell into a deep, dark hole.

The walls of the hole were too high for Small Deer to jump out. So she sat down to think.

224

Storyteller: Soon Pig came by. He looked into the dark hole and laughed.

Pig: Silly Small Deer. Why are you sitting way down there?

Storyteller: Small Deer found a big leaf. She began to look at the leaf as if she were reading something on it.

Small Deer: I am reading this Magic Leaf.

Pig: What does it say?

Small Deer: The words on the Magic Leaf say that the world will end today. Only those in the Deep Hole will be saved.

Pig: Then I will come down into the Deep Hole with you!

Small Deer: No, no! You sneeze too much, Pig.
For it says here that we must throw anyone
who sneezes out of the Deep Hole at once.

Pig: I won't sneeze. I won't even sniff.
I promise you!

Storyteller: So saying, Pig jumped down
into the Deep Hole. Small Deer went
on reading the Magic Leaf.

Storyteller: Soon Tiger came by. He looked into the Deep Hole and laughed.

Tiger: Silly animals. Why do you sit way down there?

Pig: Small Deer has read the Magic Leaf. The words on the Magic Leaf say that the world will end today. Only those in the Deep Hole will be saved.

Tiger: Then I will come down into the Deep Hole with you!

Pig: No, no! You sneeze too much, Tiger.
We must throw anyone who sneezes
out of the Deep Hole at once.

Tiger: I won't sneeze. Not even one sniffle.
I promise you!

Storyteller: So saying, Tiger jumped down
into the Deep Hole.

Storyteller: Then Elephant came by and looked into the Deep Hole.

Elephant: What are you doing down there?

Tiger: The words on the Magic Leaf say that the world will end today. Only those in the Deep Hole will be saved.

Elephant: Then I will come down there, too!

229

Tiger: No, no! You are much too big.
And you sneeze too much. We must throw
anyone who sneezes out of the Deep Hole
at once.

Elephant: I will not sniff, sniffle, or sneeze.
Here I come!

Storyteller: So saying, Elephant jumped
into the Deep Hole.

Storyteller: Small Deer went on reading
the Magic Leaf. Then she looked up.

Small Deer: Pig, are you going to sneeze?

Pig: No, no! Not I! See, I will push my nose
into the dirt so I cannot sneeze.

Storyteller: Pig pushed his nose into the dirt
and didn't sneeze. But it was very hard
for him to breathe.

Storyteller: Small Deer went on reading
the Magic Leaf. Then she looked up again.

Small Deer: Someone is about to sneeze!
Is it you, Tiger?

Tiger: No, no! Not I! See, I will hold my nose
with my paws so I cannot sneeze at all.

Storyteller: Tiger held his nose with his paws.
He didn't sneeze at all. But he
couldn't breathe very well.

Storyteller: Small Deer looked at the Magic Leaf.
Then she looked at Elephant.

Small Deer: It is you, Elephant. It is you
who will sneeze.

Elephant: No, no! Not I! I will sit on my trunk
and never sneeze one sneeze.

Storyteller: Elephant sat on her trunk
and never sneezed even one sneeze.
But she could hardly breathe at all.

Storyteller: Just then Small Deer let the leaf fall.

Her nose went up and her sides went out.

Small Deer: AHHHHH . . .

Pig: Don't sneeze, Small Deer!

Tiger and Elephant: Stop! Stop!

Storyteller: But Small Deer did not stop.

She shut her eyes and opened her mouth.

Small Deer: AHHHHH . . .

KERRR . . .

CHOOOOO!

Pig: Small Deer has sneezed!

Tiger: We must throw her out of the Deep Hole!

Elephant: At once!

Storyteller: Then the animals took hold
of Small Deer and threw her up and
out of the hole.

Storyteller: Small Deer looked down at Pig, Elephant, and Tiger.

Small Deer: Thank you, my friends. I wasn't really waiting for the world to end. But I *was* waiting to get out of this hole.

Storyteller: And with that, Small Deer went off to find some lunch.

What Does It Mean?

Here are two sentences. As you read them, decide who they tell about.

1. Helen shut her eyes. **She** began to count to one hundred.

Both sentences are about a girl named Helen. Her name was used in the first sentence. But the word She was used in the second sentence.

You knew that the two sentences went together. And you knew that the first sentence spoke of Helen. So you knew that the word She in the second sentence had to mean Helen.

1, 2, 3, 4, 5...

Words like she, he, him, them, and it
do not mean much all by themselves.
You have to look at the words around them
to find out just what they mean.

Here are some other pairs of sentences.
As you read them, decide what the words
in heavy black letters mean. Sometimes
there will be more than one of these words
in a sentence.

2. Howie came in next to last in the race.

   Only one other person came in after **him.**

   Who is meant by the word him? How did
   you know?

3. Fred and Mark could not understand
the message from Ann. **She** forgot
to give **them** a copy of the code!

Who is meant by the word She? Who is
meant by the word them? How did you know?

4. Tom and Amy took care of their
little sister. **They** took **her** to a show.

Who is meant by the word They? Who is
meant by the word her? How did you know?

Words like <u>there</u>, <u>then</u>, and <u>here</u> may also mean different things when they are used in sentences. Read each sentence below and decide what the word in heavy black letters means.

5. I thought I saw a tree frog on the trunk. But it isn't **there** now.

The word <u>there</u> means "on the trunk."

6. You mean the party isn't until Wednesday? I'm not sure I can wait until **then!**

What is meant by the word <u>then</u>? How did you know?

7. This store was full of people a minute ago. But no one is **here** now.

What is meant by the word <u>here</u>? How did you know?

Seesaw

by BONNIE NIMS

See
      saw
Up
      down
Smile
      frown
High
      low
Yes
      no
Fly
      squirm
Bird
      worm
Sky
      floor
Wave
      shore
Once more:
And
      or.

The Secret Riddle

by SID FLEISCHMAN

I hope you don't have a friend like Wally.
He lives across the street.

Wally is always playing tricks. And then
he runs around like a chicken and laughs.

One day Wally came to our door.

"Let me in, Jimmy," said Wally.

"No," I said. "My sister is sick."

"I want to tell her a riddle," said Wally.
"It will make her laugh."

I had been trying to get Kate to laugh
for days. So I let Wally in.

"Do you want to hear a riddle?"
Wally asked Kate.

"No," said Kate.

"It's a funny riddle."

"Well, all right," said Kate.

"Ready? Here's the riddle. *Dog-gone!* "

I said, "That's not a riddle!"

"It's the answer to one," said Wally.
"You've got to think of the question.
That's what makes it so funny!"

He ran around like a chicken. He laughed
all the way out of the house.

"I feel sick," said Kate.

"You're already sick," I said.

"I feel sicker. He'll never tell us the riddle."

"Maybe someone else knows it. I'll be back," I said.

I met Mr. Hunt at the front door.

"Do you know any riddles, Mr. Hunt?"
I asked.

Mr. Hunt thought a minute. "What did
the fly say when it fell into the butter?"

"Dog-gone," I answered.

"No. It said, 'Look! I'm a butterfly.' "

At the store I asked Mrs. Mitchell,
"Do you know any riddles?"

"Let me think," she said. "Oh yes.
Here's one about a clock. If you put a clock
in a beehive, what time would it be?"

"I give up," I said.

"Why, it would be hive o'clock,"
Mrs. Mitchell smiled.

I helped Mr. Snow with his bags. "Do you
know any riddles?" I asked.

"Sure I do," he answered. "If ducks say
'Quack! Quack!' when they walk, what do they
say when they run?"

"Dog-gone?" I asked.

"They say 'Quick! Quick!'" laughed Mr. Snow.

Maybe Wally had made up that silly answer
of his. But it gave me an idea. I ran back
to the store to buy a small notebook. I would
write down all the riddles before I forgot any.

Q. What did the crow say after eating Mrs. White's strawberries?

A. Thank you berry much!

Q. How did three sardines walk across the street?

A. Don't be silly. Sardines can't walk!

Q. What does a toad sit on?

A. A toad stool!

Just about everyone I met had a riddle
to tell me.

The book was almost full when I saw
Miss Smith. "Oh, I know a riddle,"
she said. "What side of a house gets
the most rain?"

"I don't know, Miss Smith," I answered.

"The outside," she said.

I wrote it down. Just then something
happened across the street. Mr. Hall's dog
got out and ran away. Mr. Hall gave a shout.

And then I laughed. Because now I knew
the question to Wally's riddle!

I wrote it in the book. On the outside
of the book, I wrote KATE'S RIDDLE BOOK.
I ran home as fast as I could.

Before long, Kate was laughing so hard
that Wally could hear her. He came
to the window.

"What are you laughing at?" he asked.

"Your riddle," said Kate. "*Dog-gone*.
Wally, that's the funniest riddle I've
ever heard."

"It is?" said Wally.

"I can't stop laughing," said Kate.

"Tell me the first part," asked Wally.

"Oh, you know the first part," said Kate.

"No, I don't," said Wally. "I just
made up the answer *dog-gone* to be funny.
I don't know the question."

"You're just saying that," laughed Kate.
"Oh, it's so funny. But don't worry.
Jimmy and I promise to keep it a secret."

"Come on and tell me," said Wally.

"You're looking kind of sick, Wally,"
said Kate. "You'd better go home to bed.
Good-by. I'm feeling so much better."

She held up the book and read
the last riddle again.

Q. What do you say
when your dog
runs away?

A. Dog-gone!

(Don't tell Wally.)

Riddles and Things

Some ABC's are hidden in this picture.
There are three A's, four B's, and ten C's.
Can you find all of them?

The Garden

by ARNOLD LOBEL

Frog was in his garden.

Toad came walking by.

"What a fine garden you have, Frog,"
he said.

"Yes," said Frog. "It is very nice,
but it was hard work."

"I wish I had a garden," said Toad.

"Here are some flower seeds. Plant them in the ground," said Frog, "and soon you will have a garden."

"How soon?" asked Toad.

"Quite soon," said Frog.

Toad ran home.

He planted the flower seeds.

"Now, seeds," said Toad, "start growing."

Toad walked up and down a few times.

The seeds did not start to grow.

Toad put his head close
to the ground and
said loudly, "Now, seeds,
start growing!"

Toad looked at the ground again.

The seeds did not start to grow.

Toad put his head very close to the ground and shouted, "NOW, SEEDS, START GROWING!"

Frog came running up the path.

"What is all this noise?" he asked.

"My seeds will not grow," said Toad.

"You are shouting too much," said Frog. "Those poor seeds are afraid to grow."

"My seeds are afraid to grow?" asked Toad.

"Of course," said Frog. "Leave them alone for a few days. Let the sun shine on them, let the rain fall on them. Soon your seeds will start to grow."

That night Toad looked out of his window. "Drat!" said Toad. "My seeds have not started to grow. They must be afraid of the dark."

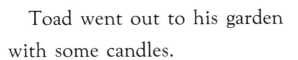

Toad went out to his garden
with some candles.

"I will read the seeds a story," said Toad.
"Then they will not be afraid."

Toad read a long story to his seeds.

All the next day Toad sang songs
to his seeds.

And all the next day Toad read poems
to his seeds.

And all the next day Toad played music
for his seeds.

Toad looked at the ground.

The seeds still did not start to grow.

"What shall I do?" cried Toad.
"These must be the most frightened seeds
in the whole world!"

Then Toad felt very tired, and he
fell asleep.

"Toad, Toad, wake up," said Frog.
"Look at your garden!"

Toad looked at his garden.

Little green plants were coming up
out of the ground.

"At last," shouted Toad, "my seeds have
stopped being afraid to grow!"

"And now you will have
a nice garden, too," said Frog.

"Yes," said Toad, "but you
were right, Frog. It was
very hard work."

Books to Enjoy

Frog and Toad All Year by Arnold Lobel
Two very good friends have fun doing all kinds of things together.

A Mad Wet Hen and Other Riddles
by Joseph Low
Here are some riddles to keep you guessing.

Too Short Fred by Susan Meddaugh
Fred is small, but he has a lot of great ideas.

Madge's Magic Show by Mike Thaler
Something funny happens when Madge tries to pull a rabbit out of a hat.

Pelly and Peak by Sally Wittman
In these stories, you will laugh at the ways two birds surprise each other.

Sounds You Know — Consonants

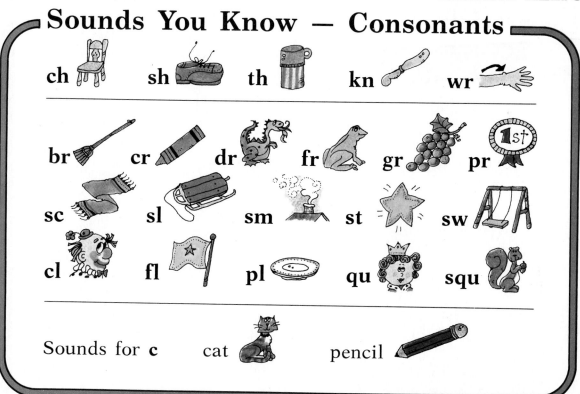

ch **sh** **th** **kn** **wr**

br **cr** **dr** **fr** **gr** **pr**

sc **sl** **sm** **st** **sw**

cl **fl** **pl** **qu** **squ**

Sounds for **c**   cat   pencil

New Sounds — Consonants

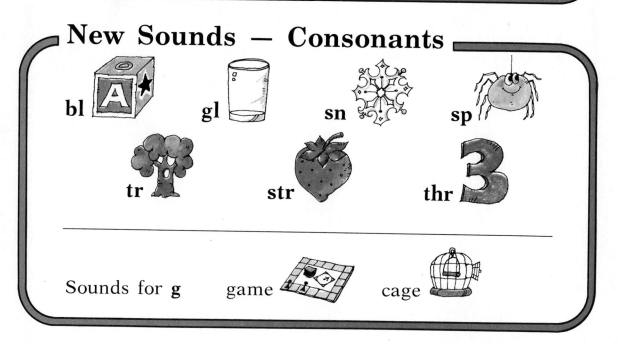

bl **gl** **sn** **sp**

tr **str** **thr**

Sounds for **g**   game   cage

Turn the page.

Sounds You Know — Vowels

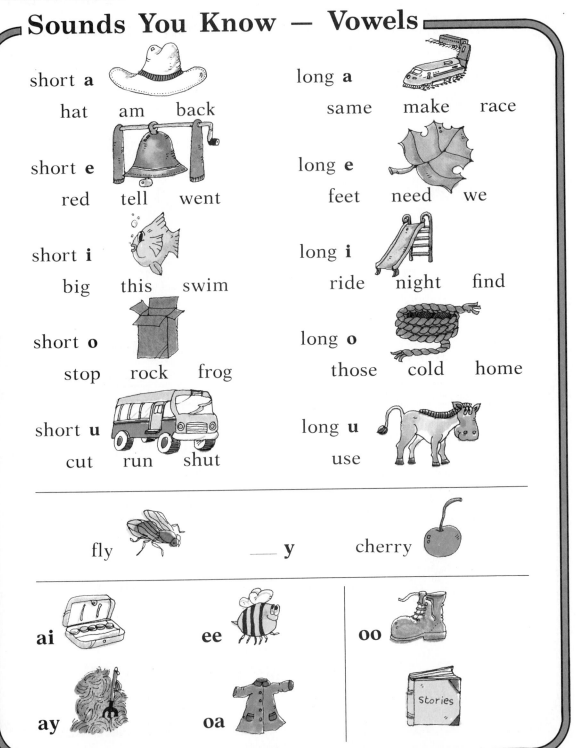

short **a**

hat   am   back

long **a**

same   make   race

short **e**

red   tell   went

long **e**

feet   need   we

short **i**

big   this   swim

long **i**

ride   night   find

short **o**

stop   rock   frog

long **o**

those   cold   home

short **u**

cut   run   shut

long **u**

use

fly   _____ **y**   cherry

ai   **ee**   **oo**

ay   **oa**

New Sounds — Vowels

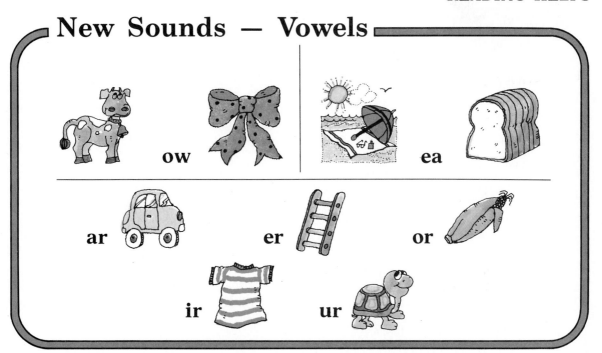

ow

ea

ar

er

or

ir

ur

When you come to a new word —

> Read to the end of the sentence.
>
> Think about what the sentence is saying.
>
> Think about the sounds letters stand for.

Does the word you named make sense in the sentence?

Does the word you named have the right sounds?

271

"Good Lemonade," from *Good Lemonade,* by Frank Asch. All Rights Reserved. Used by permission of the publisher, Franklin Watts, Inc.

"Grownups Are Funny," adapted from "Grown-Ups Are Funny," from *Junk Day on Juniper Street,* by Lilian Moore. Text copyright © 1969 by Lilian Moore. Used by permission of Parents' Magazine Press.

"The House That Nobody Wanted," adapted from "The House That Nobody Wanted," from *Junk Day on Juniper Street,* by Lilian Moore. Text copyright © 1969 by Lilian Moore. Used by permission of Parents' Magazine Press.

"I Love Gram," from *I Love Gram,* by Ruth A. Sonneborn. Copyright © Ruth A. Sonneborn, 1971. All rights reserved. Reprinted by permission of Viking Penguin Inc.

"Impossible, Possum," adaptation of *Impossible, Possum,* by Ellen Conford. Text Copyright © 1971 by Ellen Conford. Illustrations Copyright © 1971 by Rosemary Wells. Used by permission of Little, Brown and Co.

"More Potatoes," adapted from *More Potatoes!* by Millicent E. Selsam. Copyright © 1972 by Millicent E. Selsam. Used by permission of Harper & Row, Publishers, Inc., and the author.

"Point of View," from *Odds Without Ends,* by David McCord. Copyright 1951 by David McCord. Originally appeared in *The Atlantic.* Reprinted by permission of Little, Brown and Co.

"The Rabbit and the Turnip," translated by Richard Sadler. English text © 1968 by Richard Sadler Ltd., Publishers. Used by permission of Richard Sadler.

"Riddles and Things," ("How does a hippo . . ."), from *The Electric Radish and Other Jokes,* selected by Susan Thorndike. Copyright © 1973 by Ray Cruz. Adapted by permission of Doubleday & Company, Inc.

"Riddles and Things," ("How many balls of string . . ."), from *5 Men Under 1 Umbrella and Other Ready-to-Read Riddles,* by Joseph Low. Copyright © 1975, by Joseph Low. Reprinted by permission of Macmillan Publishing Co., Inc. British rights granted by World's Work Ltd.

"Riddles and Things," ("What four letters . . ."), adapted from *Funny Jokes and Foxy Riddles,* by Allan Jaffee. © 1968 by Western Publishing Company, Inc. Used by permission of the publisher.

"The Secret Hiding Place," adapted from *The Secret Hiding Place,* by Rainey Bennett. Copyright © 1960 by Rainey Bennett. Adapted with the permission of William Collins Publishers, Inc.

"The Secret Riddle," adapted from *Kate's Secret Riddle Book,* by Albert S. Fleischman. Text Copyright © 1977 by Albert S. Fleischman. Used by permission of the publisher, Franklin Watts, Inc. and Curtis Brown, Ltd.

"Seesaw," by Bonnie Nims. Excerpted from the book *I Wish I Lived at the Playground,* copyright © 1972 by Bonnie Nims. Published by J. Philip O'Hara, Inc. Reprinted by permission of the author.

"Small Deer's Magic Leaf," adapted from *Small Deer's Magic Tricks,* by Betty Boegehold. Copyright © 1977 by Betty Boegehold. Adapted by permission of Coward, McCann, and Geoghegan, Inc.

"The Talking Tiger," from *A Lion I Can Do Without,* by Arnold Spilka. Copyright 1964 by Arnold Spilka. Reprinted by permission of the author.

"What I'd Like," by Lee Blair (pseudonym for Leland B. Jacobs) from *Arithmetic in Verse and Rhyme,* selected by Allan D. Jacobs and Leland B. Jacobs. Published by Garrard Publishing Company, 1971. Reprinted by permission of Leland B. Jacobs.

"A Window," from *Photographs and Poems by Sioux Children,* published by Indian Arts and Crafts Board, United States Department of the Interior. Reprinted with their permission and the permission of Arthur Amiotte.

"The Wizard of Wallaby Wallow," adapted from *The Wizard of Wallaby Wallow,* by Jack Kent. Text Copyright © 1971 by Jack Kent. Illustration Copyright © 1971 by Jack Kent. Used by permission of Parents' Magazine Press.

Credits

Illustrators: pp. 7–14, JURG FURRER; pp. 20–21, LYNN MUNSINGER; pp. 22–31, EULALA CONNER; pp. 32–33, KAZUE MIZUMURA; pp. 34–37, 69–72, 115–117, 168–170, 202–205, 237–239, LANE YERKES; pp. 38–46, JAN BRETT; p. 47, SEYMOUR SIMMONS III; pp. 48–65, MONICA ANAGANASTORAS; pp. 66, 87–93, DORTHEA SIERRA; p. 68, LARRY JOHNSON; pp. 73–82, DIANE DAWSON; pp. 94–97, GARY FUJIWARA; pp. 98–111, JUDY LOVE; pp. 112–113, SAS COLBY; pp. 118–139, ROSEMARY WELLS; pp. 140–149, PENNY CARTER; pp. 150–151, JACK REILLY; pp. 152–167, WILLI BAUM; p. 171, BARI WEISSMAN; pp. 172–183, ANNIE GUSMAN; p. 184, ANNIE BUTTE; pp. 189–200, JACK KENT; p. 201, LINDA BICK; p. 206, SALLY MAVOR; pp. 207–217, SUSAN LEXA; pp. 218–221, JOAN PALEY; p. 222, LYDIA DOBCOVICH; pp. 223–235, MONICA SANTA; p. 241, ANGELA ADAMS; pp. 242–255, DAVE BLANCHETTE; pp. 256–257, GORDON KIBBEE; pp. 258–266, ARNOLD LOBEL.

Photographers: p. 15, J. D. CUNNINGHAM; p. 16, STAN WAYMAN/Photo Researchers (P.R.); p. 17 top, bottom, LEONARD LEE RUE/National Audubon Society (N.A.S.); p. 17 middle, KEN BRATE/P.R.; p. 18 left, S. J. KRASEMANN/P.R.; p. 18 right, CHARLIE OTT/N.A.S.; p. 19, COSMOS BLANK/N.A.S.; p. 66 top, J. ALSOP/Bruce Coleman Inc.; p. 66 bottom, FREDERICK AYER/P.R.; p. 67 left, Grant Heilman Inc.; p. 67 middle, © JACK WILBURN/Earth Scenes; p. 67 right, DR. E. R. DEGGINGER; pp. 87–93, CAROL PALMER, ANDY BRILLIANT; p. 94 left, JAMES H. KARALES/Peter Arnold Inc.; p. 94 right, JOHN COLWELL/Grant Heilman Inc.; p. 95, 96 bottom, 97, BOHDAN HRYNEWICH; p. 96 top, ERIK ANDERSON/Stock Boston; pp. 112–113, 206, DEIRDRA STEAD.

Book cover, title page, and magazine covers by KRYSTYNA STASIAK.

272